"The great nations couldn't but envy the power, wealth, prudence, and continued success of Venice. With less than three million subjects and a territorial extension less than one-tenth of France, Venice reached the height of the greatest empires."

Jean Charles Leonard de Sismondi
nineteenth-century Swiss historian

VENICESCAPES

Reference Guide

Story of a
Mercantile Empire

text and original historical maps
contributed by
Jarrod Michael Broderick

Official patronage
of the
Venice Board of Tourism

Developed for
VENICESCAPES
http://www.venicescapes.org

Cover
Venice, Ducal Palace by Sam Prout
Steel engraving by Westwood, 1836.

Copyright © by VENICESCAPES 2000, 2010
All Rights Reserved

Contents

Map of the Roman Empire in AD 395   1
with successive barbarian invasions

Map of the Byzantine Empire and   2
Barbarian Kingdoms in AD 526

Map of the Byzantine Empire and   3
Frankish Kingdoms in AD 565

Map of Maritime Venice in AD 751   4
with the principle settlements
and the mainland cities of origin

Map of the Western Roman and   5
Byzantine Empires in AD 811

VENETO-BYZANTINE   6

Map of the Norman Conquests   8
in Southern Italy as of AD 1091
with the maximum extension of Venice's territories
in Istria, Dalmatia, and Albania

Map of the Crusader States in AD 1113   9
with the principle caravan routes

Map of the Latin Empire in AD 1211   10
with the maximum extension of Venice's
territories and feuds in the Levant

Map of the Maximum Expansion and   11
Division of the Mongol Empire
with the probable routes of Niccolò, Maffeo, and Marco Polo

GOTHIC   12

Map of the Venetian Merchant   14
Galley Fleets in the 15th Century
with the centers of the principle European fairs

Map of Venice's Mainland   15
Territories in AD 1509
with the principle routes to the Alpine passes

EARLY RENAISSANCE   16

"ROMAN" RENAISSANCE   18

Map of the Ottoman Empire in AD 1699   20

Map of the Oceanic Trade Routes   21
in the 17th and 18th Centuries
with the English, French, Portughese, and Dutch colonies

BAROQUE   22

PALLADIAN AND NEOCLASSICAL   24

Map of the Unification of Italy   26
with the national borders as of AD 1954

Notes   27

Geologic Formation   Appendix
of the Italian Peninsula

STORY OF A
MERCANTILE
EMPIRE

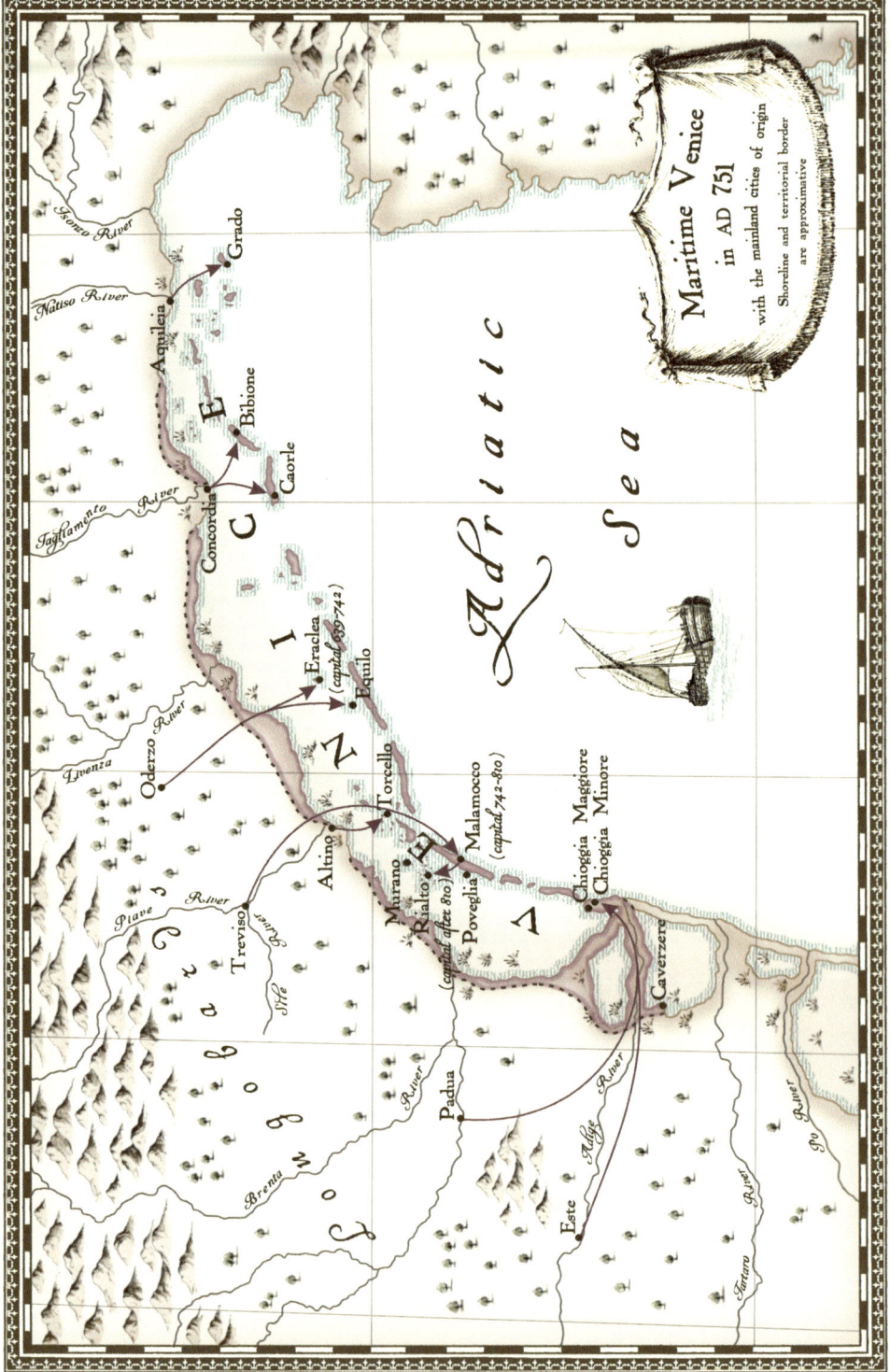

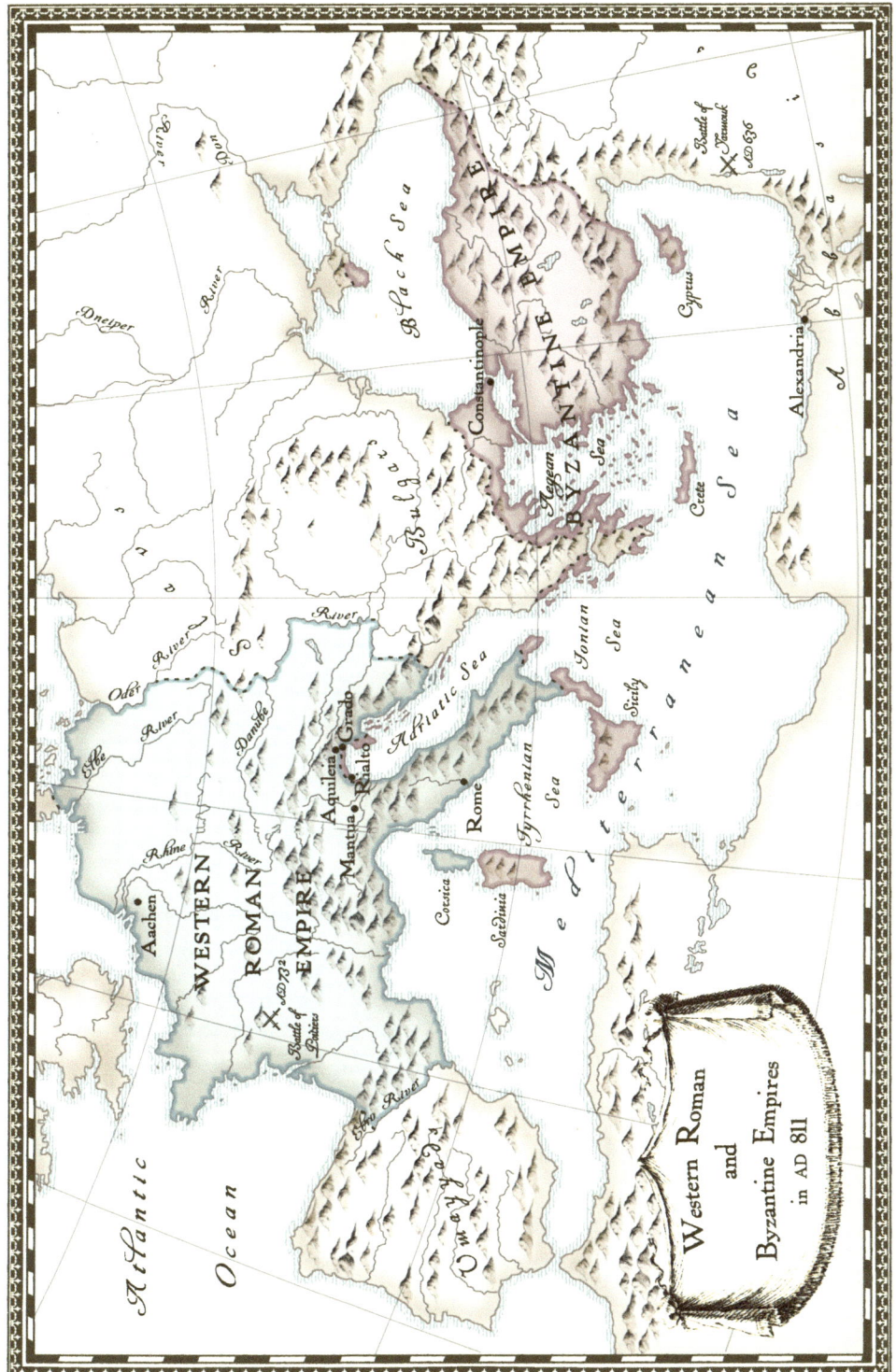

VENETO-BYZANTINE

Of the primitive dwellings built on the marshy islands of the Venetian Lagoon, nothing remains. Limited local building materials and the difficulty of constructing on the unstable, sandy soil made it necessary to erect simple wooden homes with thatched roofs which have long since been cancelled by time and the urbanization of later centuries. Early churches, built on higher, more stable ground using the brick and stone salvaged from the ruins of the mainland cities, are consequently the oldest surviving examples of Venetian architecture. Initially resembling the cathedrals of Aquileia and Altinum that had been abandoned when the original refugees fled towards the sea, these churches began to show a stronger eastern influence as Venetian merchants took increasing advantage of trading privileges within the Byzantine Empire and funds became available to modernize or replace the original buildings. Arches were heightened with slender columns and gradually assumed the aspect of the Byzantine stilted arch as the sense of order and clarity inherent in the paleo-Christian architecture of the West gave way to the complicated interiors typical of the giant, Greek-cross churches of Constantinople.

Decorative preferences also felt the impact of the growing commercial ties with both the Byzantine and Islamic worlds. Shimmering glass and gold mosaics and precious oriental marbles soon covered the originally stark interiors, imbuing them with an aura of eastern mysticism, while the austere brick facades, already accented with locally available Istrian stone, were further enriched with the addition of sculptural fragments stripped by sailors, merchants, and pilgrims from ancient ruins in the East. Lacking the relief of classical Roman statuary which would inspire many of the developments in western architecture, these "trophies" established instead the long-standing Venetian tradition of elaborate, two-dimensional surface decoration.

By the twelfth and thirteenth centuries brick and stone had also been introduced into domestic construction as the city's wealthier merchants were by this point in the financial position to begin erecting large family palaces to provide both suitable living quarters as well as the spaces necessary for the storage of merchandise and the direction of their increasingly complex and lucrative trading activities. Inspired by the

Arab *fondouk*, or trading post, and supported by a network of wooden piles driven into the sandy soil, these homes provided the basic building type and floor plan of future Venetian palaces while the facades, open to allow for the loading and unloading of wares and the maximum penetration of natural light into the dark, inner recesses, soon became vehicles to express the wealth and tastes of the individual owners. Medallions, relief sculpture, and red porphyries imported from the East were incorporated between the successive bays of stilted arches which throughout the remainder of the Byzantine period slowly acquired the pointed Islamic forms that would give rise to the distinctly Venetian version of Gothic.

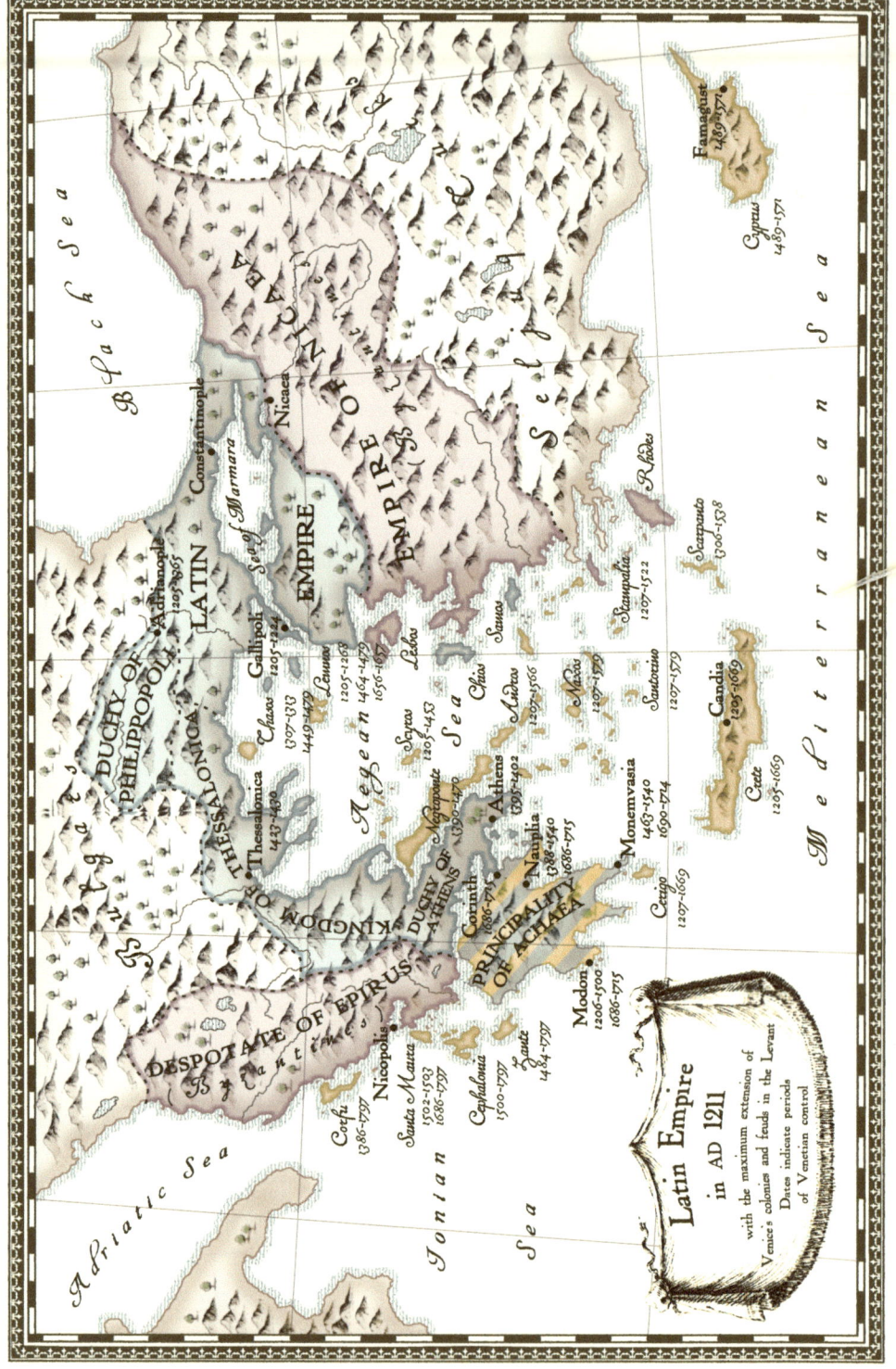

GOTHIC

Venice reached the apex of its political and commercial power during the fourteenth and fifteenth centuries. Great expansion in overseas commerce and the implementation of aggressive mercantile laws aimed at ensuring Venetian dominance of the Levantine trade resulted in the accumulation of vast fortunes in the hands of the city's noble-mercantile families which undertook the construction of lavishly decorated palaces to express their growing wealth and status.

Although the Republic had by this time begun to expand its dominion over the Italian mainland, it remained essentially a seafaring nation with predominant commercial and cultural ties in the East. Artistic tastes consequently continued to reflect the travels of merchants, sailors, and pilgrims. Elaborate crenalations inspired by Egyptian mosques crowned a greater number of rooflines; inlaid tiles reproduced Persian designs; and delicately carved Moorish traceries took the form of balconies or flowed in intricate arabesque patterns above the increasingly pointed windows. Facades were largely frescoed or alternatively covered with a brick-red stucco containing marble dust which glittered under the bright sun and glistened in the ripples on the surface of the canals while gold and polychrome decoration was added and the white Istrian stone touched up with white lead and oiled to look like gleaming marble.

Substantially, the floor plan inherited from the Veneto-Byzantine period remained unaltered with the wide, central hall helping to illuminate those inner rooms that received even less light as a result of the densely built-up urban environment. But the open loggia typical of Veneto-Byzantine waterfront palaces had by this time been reduced to a large window grouping in correspondence to the central hall giving rise to the characteristic tripartite design of Venetian facades.

Religious buildings, in contrast, underwent a radical structural change at the beginning of the thirteenth century with the arrival in the city of the recently established mendicant orders. Internationally organized and administered, these orders, foremost of which the Dominicans and Franciscans, introduced into Venice their own building designs as they had already begun to evolve outside the unique Venetian context. With

a sense of soaring space and divine light and vast naves wherein the city's growing urban population could seek spiritual consolation, the huge, new churches made a deep impression on Venetian religious sensibilities, and by the fourteenth century, the small, centrally planned Veneto-Byzantine parish churches had given way to simple, triple-naved Gothic churches in emulation of those of the mendicant orders. To a far lesser extent, the new churches also affected secular construction. The inherent decorative elements provided new visual ideas, and soon quatrefoils and the solid, uninflected arch appeared in domestic buildings where they harmonized perfectly with the inflected arches and elaborate traceries of Islamic origin.

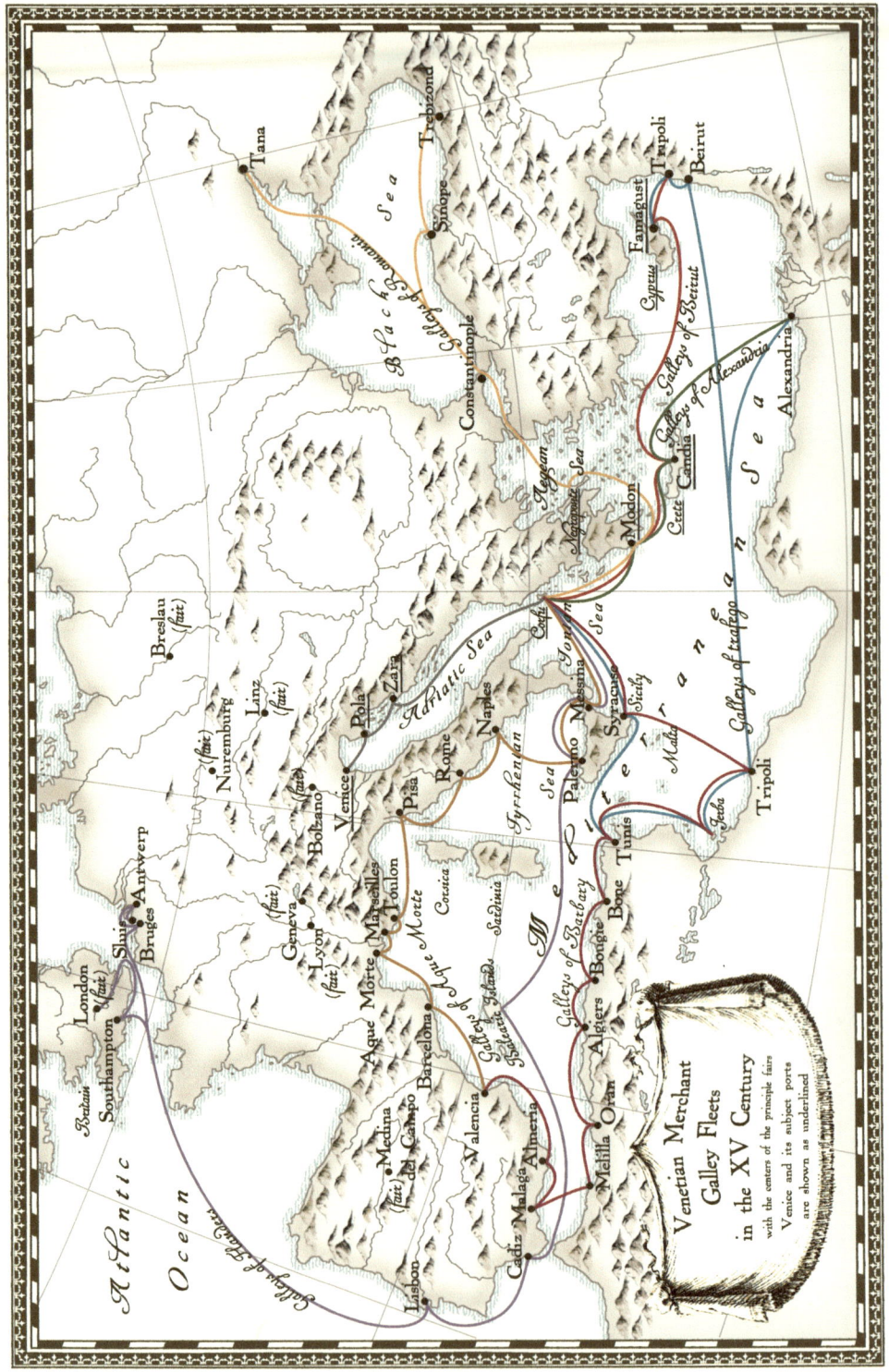

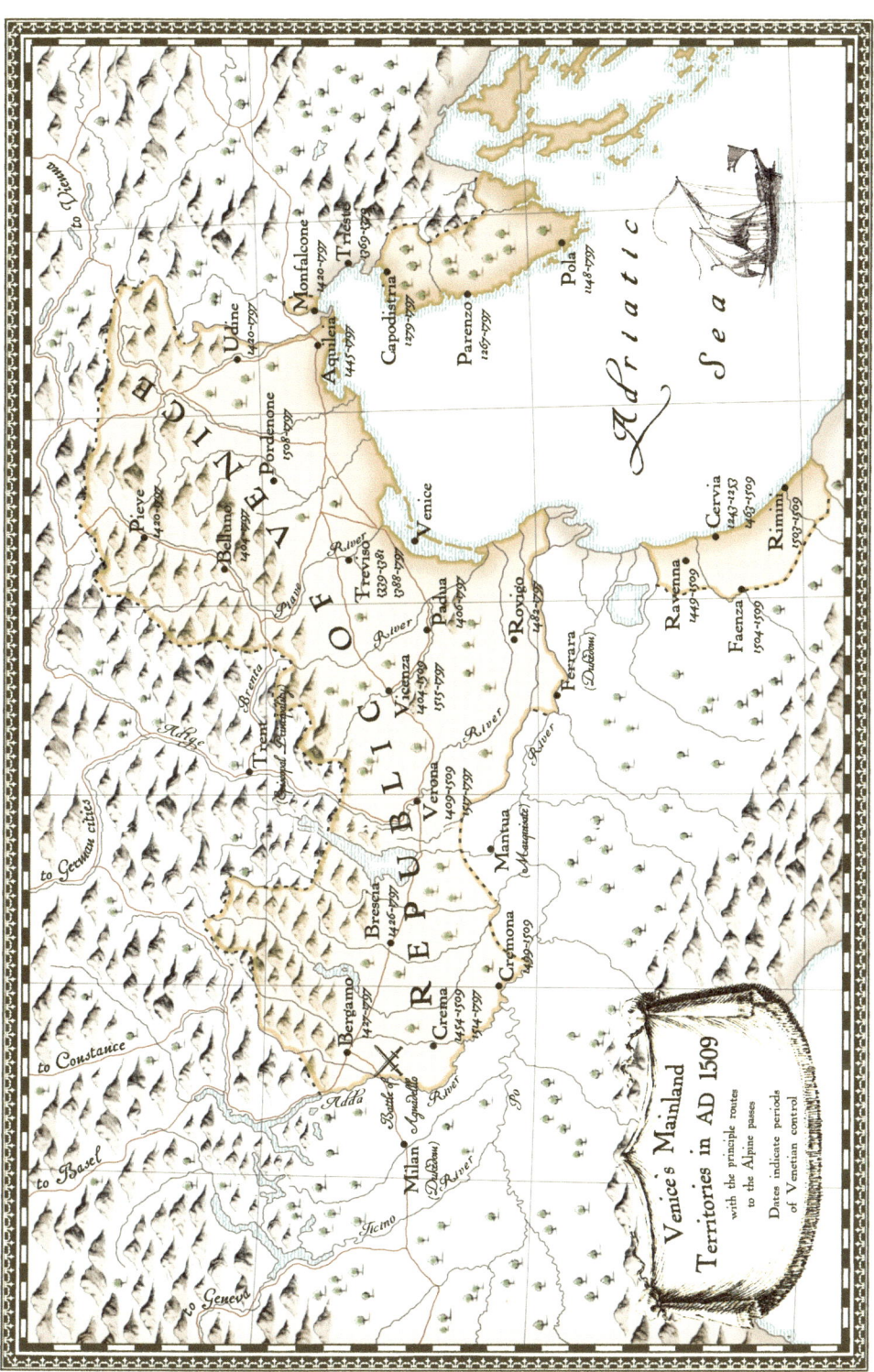

EARLY RENAISSANCE

Venice's expansion on the Italian mainland during the fifteenth century brought the Venetians into increasing contact with the artistic ideas of the Florentine Renaissance, but their impact on the city's architecture was slow due to the deeply rooted cultural ties in the East, the lack of nearby Roman ruins to inspire local builders, and the growing political tensions between Venice and Florence which ultimately resulted in the expulsion of the Florentines in 1440. Yet frequent visits by Tuscan architects to the Lombardy continued to influence the designs of northern Italian artisans, and soon the stonemasons and sculptors from Milan, Bergamo, and Como who routinely worked in Venice had indirectly introduced the *all'antica* decorative elements inherent in Tuscan architecture. Although arbitrarily applied to traditional Venetian tripartite facades, these Renaissance motifs nevertheless created a more classical appearance while the extensive use of relief sculpture and colored marbles continued to respect the Venetian predilection for chromatic effects and elaborately ornamented surfaces.

The city's religious orders, in contrast, proved once again receptive to the more radical of the new ideas. With ties to their fellow communities on the Italian mainland and a tradition of academic studies, they understood far more of the underlying Renaissance principles of coherence, balance, and harmony. Their churches, conceived in emulation of the buildings of antiquity with a restrained use of ornamentation to organize and explain the entire structure rather than simply decorate it, constitute as a result the first true examples of Renaissance architecture in Venice.

Inspired by these churches, builders looked increasingly toward central Italy for visual ideas, and largely through the work of Mauro Codussi, a stonemason from Bergamo, the Florentine prototypes were adapted to suit Venice's physical conditions and the new principles finally integrated into local building traditions. Round-arched Tuscan windows were conceived on a larger scale to allow for the greater penetration of light while the white Istrian stone – for centuries confined to details such as balconies, doorways, and window frames – began to be employed for entire facades due to its potential to create striking, classical effects.

With a keen understanding of the logic behind Renaissance architecture and great ingenuity, Codussi revolutionized both secular and religious construction in Venice and created some of the more dignified buildings of the early Italian Renaissance, but his highly original ideas did not have an immediate effect on the development of Venetian architecture. Following his death in 1504, hostilities broke out between Venice and the League of Cambrai for the control of the recently acquired mainland cities. An acute financial crisis ensued which stifled artistic ideas and limited construction to indispensable government structures or heavily endowed religious buildings erected in spite of wartime restraints as a means of invoking divine aid.

"ROMAN" RENAISSANCE

Venice's financial recovery after the traumatic period of the Cambrai wars coincided with the sack of in 1527 and the Venetians' consequent desire to create a "New Rome" on their own soil. With its origins reaching back to the fall of the Roman Empire and a government modeled along the lines of the Roman Republic, Venice had in fact long considered itself as Rome's truest successor. In the same period, the publication in Venice of Vitruvius' "*De architectura*" and the arrival in the city of Sebastiano Serlio and Jacopo Sansovino, both of whom had fled from the papal court following the sack, gave the Venetians the inspiration and the expertise necessary to recreate authentic Roman architectural forms.

Serlio's contribution to the new style was purely academic. He published two important volumes with a range of visual ideas based on ancient Roman architecture as well as details for the proportions of columns, capitals, and architraves. Although he soon left Venice to go to France, his "Serliana" tripartite window became a popular solution in sixteenth-century Venetian palaces for lighting the large central halls.

The Florentine-born Jacopo Sansovino, unlike Serlio, remained in Venice. A sculptor by training, he was instinctively a versatile architect, and in the end, his work came to epitomize the Venetian concept of "Roman" architecture. While successfully employing classical motifs, well-proportioned columns, and friezes, Sansovino managed to respect two long-standing Venetian traditions. His abundant use of statues and carvings seemed to continue the Venetian passion for collecting classical sculpture and applying it to existing buildings while his tendency toward a dominant shadow-and-light effect, which could be achieved with deeply recessed windows and richly embellished walls, responded to the Venetian penchant for surface decoration.

While Sansovino ensured his long success and popularity by incorporating aspects of the local building traditions into his work, Andrea Palladio, the most gifted and important architect of the period, was far too innovative to meet with the approval of Venice's conservative aristocratic government. The brilliant Paduan-born architect was denied the position of State architect in 1554 and

repeatedly saw many of his designs for official buildings rejected in favor of more traditional solutions. As typically occurred in Venice, the city's religious orders, and not the government, embraced the bold new ideas. His principle buildings in the city are consequently monastic and conventual churches which together with the numerous villas built for Venice's patrician families on the Italian mainland, would eventually inspire the Palladian style in seventeenth-century England and make Palladio one of the more important architects in European history. With their imposing, white facades, these churches also gave a new monumentality to Venetian architecture and prepared the way for the more triumphant Baroque.

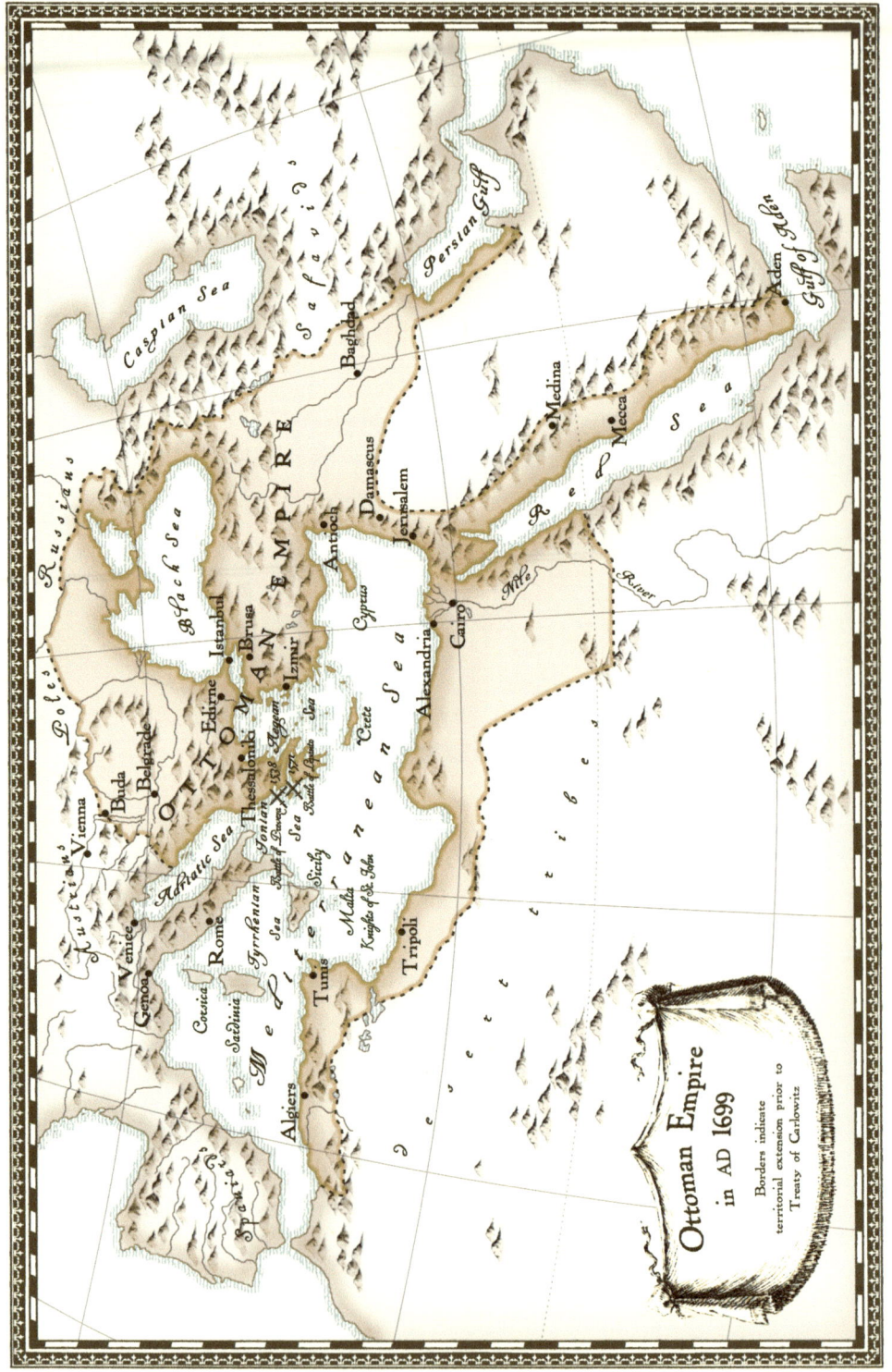

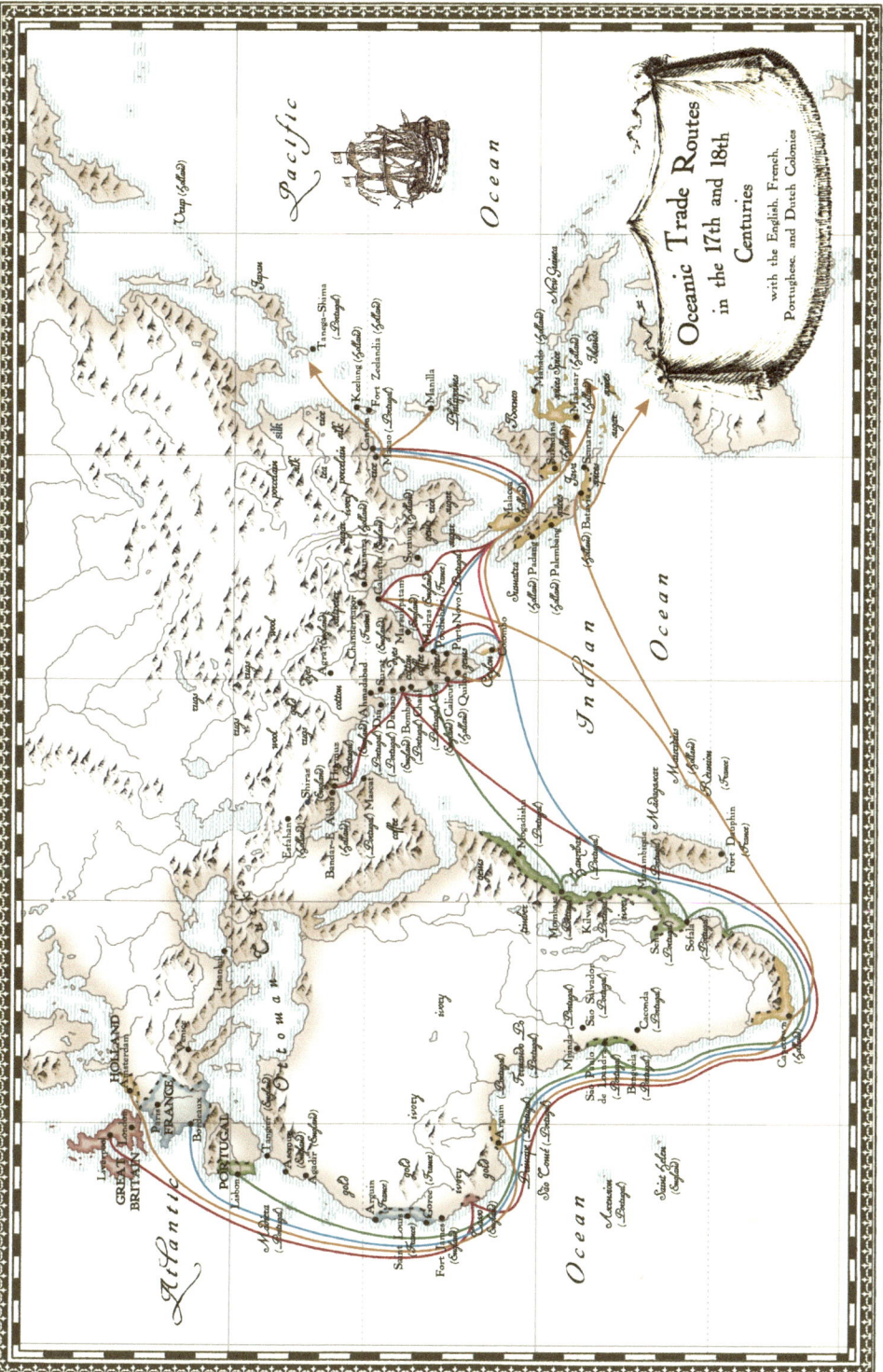

BAROQUE

By the seventeenth century, Venice was following western Europe's architectural trends and tastes. Throughout the preceding century, ties with the subject territories on the Italian mainland had been strengthened when heavy investments in agriculture were made in order to free the Republic from both the effects of the rapidly rising prices of imported wheat as well as the economic uncertainty of conducting overseas trade in waters subject to piracy, storms, and the ongoing wars against the Turks. The city's economy, while no longer centered on trade with the Levant, knew moments of prosperity in this period due primarily to the flourishing domestic textile industry, and this created the sense of renewed confidence in Venice and its future that the bold and triumphant Baroque style seemed to embody.

Architectural preferences in the city began to show signs of the new style's influence in the latter decades of the sixteenth century although the great wealth required to implement it on a suitably grand scale restricted it to State initiative and the city's wealthier families. In more modest dwellings, animal masks, fanciful balustrades, and other decorative elements simply filtered down and were incorporated with more-or-less success into traditional Venetian facades.

Remarkably, the city's Byzantine heritage provided a wealth of visual ideas that had a particular affinity with the flamboyant new style. The rhythmic alternation of dark, cavernous spaces and vast surfaces typical of Byzantine architecture demonstrated that geometrical forms and interconnected spaces could be manipulated to achieve dramatic results. Also, the glittering white Istrian stone, the city's traditional building material, was ideal for achieving the majestic, scenographic effects inherent in Baroque while the microscopic mildew that naturally forms on the candid surfaces wherever niches and recesses protect it from rain and sun made it possible to obtain the characteristic Baroque interplay between shadow and light.

It was in the work of Baldassare Longhena that these traditions were completely exploited, and the style reached its full potential to express Venice's renewed self-confidence. Avoiding the emotional and

theological manipulation typical in the architecture of post-Tridentine Rome, Longhena directed his technical ingenuity and artistic sensibilities to creating a highly personal form of Baroque — characterized by a restrained use of decorative elements — which nevertheless produced striking visual effects while responding to the Venetian sensibilities toward light and space. His buildings, foremost of which the great votive temple of Santa Maria della Salute, erected to invoke the city's deliverance from the terrible pestilence of 1630-1631, at times even rival those of his Roman contemporaries and clearly distinguish him as the pre-eminent Baroque architect in the whole of northern Italy.

PALLADIAN AND NEOCLASSICAL

Throughout Europe, the early eighteenth century was characterized by an overt contrast between confidence in mankind's scientific and technological progress and apprehension for the unknown world that the resulting Age of Enlightenment was to usher in, and as the century advanced, architecture increasingly reflected this dualist mood. Nostalgia for the certainties of a lost, "golden" way of life led to the frivolity of Rococo with its swaying forms and elegance while the continued quest for knowledge tended more toward a rational and austere style that seemed both to reflect the growing interest in the study of the arts and sciences as well as impose order on an apparently fragile world.

In Venice, the Rococo sense of playfulness had an impact chiefly on interiors which came to reflect the general desire to escape from the realities of a bankrupt treasury and the first rumblings of political discontent whereas the architecture of the period was largely devoid of the characteristic Rococo delicacy that pervaded much of Europe. Instead, a growing need for a solid, reassuring style to counterbalance the doubts about the Republic's future induced local architects to seek inspiration in the sober, more classical forms inherited from Palladio.

Church facades, funded primarily by those recently admitted members of the aristocracy who yearned to glorify their own reputations, became the principle vehicles to express the new trend since neither the government nor the vast majority of the city's ancient noble families remained in the economic position to finance public buildings or private palaces. Slowly, the crowning statuary and broken pediments of Baroque disappeared; sculpture was reduced to statues neatly arranged in niches or limited to relief panels; and the few Rococo decorative elements initially adopted by local architects were purged.

By the middle of the eighteenth century, the tendency toward simpler, more linear forms had brought European architecture into harmony with the rational Enlightenment spirit and led to the Neoclassical style. For Venice, the transition came almost effortlessly, simply continuing the trend already initiated with the Palladian revival. Non-functional decorative elements were now virtually rejected in conformity with the

most radical of the international currents of thought, and flat walls came to play an increasingly important role in the overall design with no attempt to mask them behind an encrustation of statues, columns, medallions, or colored inserts in the Venetian tradition. The city's architects also began to seek inspiration among the most dignified models of antiquity for the few constructions that the depressed economy permitted in these waning years of the Republic and, for the first time, to nurture an admiration for the buildings of Ancient Greece which despite the centuries of commercial contacts within the Greek world had never directly influenced the city's architecture.

Notes

Notes

Notes

Notes

Notes

Notes

Appendix

Geologic Formation of the Italian Peninsula

THE ITALIAN PENINSULA DURING
THE PLIOCENE EPOCH 4.5 - 4 MILLION YEARS AGO

(City names indicate future sites)

THE ITALIAN PENINSULA DURING
THE WÜRM GLACIATION 18,000 YEARS AGO

(City names indicate future sites)